SUBLIMISM

INDEX

Nathan Coppedge

SUBLIMISM

Nathan Coppedge

SUBLIMISM

By Nathan Coppedge

Nathan Coppedge

SUBLIMISM

INTRODUCTION

Largely the question of beauty is the question of the sublime: the question of the ultimate realization of beauty, the most original or most natural form of art. While there is some question of its subjectivity, most audiences agree that beauty --- not just artistic beauty, but poetic or logical beauty ---- is open to certain classifications. Whatever classification happens to be used, it is that classification by which such art is held to a sublime standard. The sublime standard is either realized or unrealized. This is often explained in terms of a rationale. What does not have a formal purpose has a diversionary purpose. What does not have a diversionary purpose has a historical purpose. And what does not have a historical purpose must still be 'art for art's sake'.

Nathan Coppedge

In this text I am considering several forms of beauty. Not just artistic beauty, although I will consider that first, but also architectural, moral, and poetic forms of beauty.

The difference in basic content means that each area demands its own criteria for the realization of the paradigm. Where the artistic sublime may easily concern natural variation, and natural beauty, poetic beauty concerns the ability to evoke beauty in the first place, and also a specific ability to evoke a sublime form of that beauty. While again, it may be up to subjective opinion, it is also true that some poetry is more intellectual, more professionally made, and more trunchent in its images than other poetry. Thus, in my examples, I follow the tradition of Emily Dickinson, Pablo Neruda, William Blake, Samuel S.T. Coleridge, e.e. cummings, and Theodore Roethke.

SUBLIMISM

In the case of the brief sections on the architectural and moral sublime, I will resort to further devices to explain how beauty might be possible at all.

In the case of architecture, beauty comes through highly specific formulas --- more specific than in the case of the visual arts. While some of the themes are similar, the result is necessarily more formal. As any architect knows, designing without design is futile, and painterly techniques are not so feasible in architecture. So, I adopt curvilinear forms, but also a modularized mentality. The key, then, is to find sublimity within the module.

In the case of moral sublimes, one must go even further, and say that morals concerns a formality that wouldn't necessarily be obvious to anyone. Even calling morality formal may be risking a break in the appropriate paradigm.

Nathan Coppedge

SUBLIMISM

ART

Nathan Coppedge

SUBLIMISM

SUBLIME ART

Sublime art concerns not just those forms which are sublime in the abstract, but those *compositions* which are without everything but the sublime.

Thus, beginning with curvilinear shapes or elements of nature is but the barest hint of the ultimate technique that is necessary to create the overall effect.

One might say that photography is a cheat. And, being a cheat, it is to be avoided. Like all cheats, it compromises the rigor of the composition. Remember, just because a photograph is successful does not mean it is the fin d' siècle of the sublime.

Indeed, sublime art requires considerable 'art'. It is as if it only happens as a work of nature...

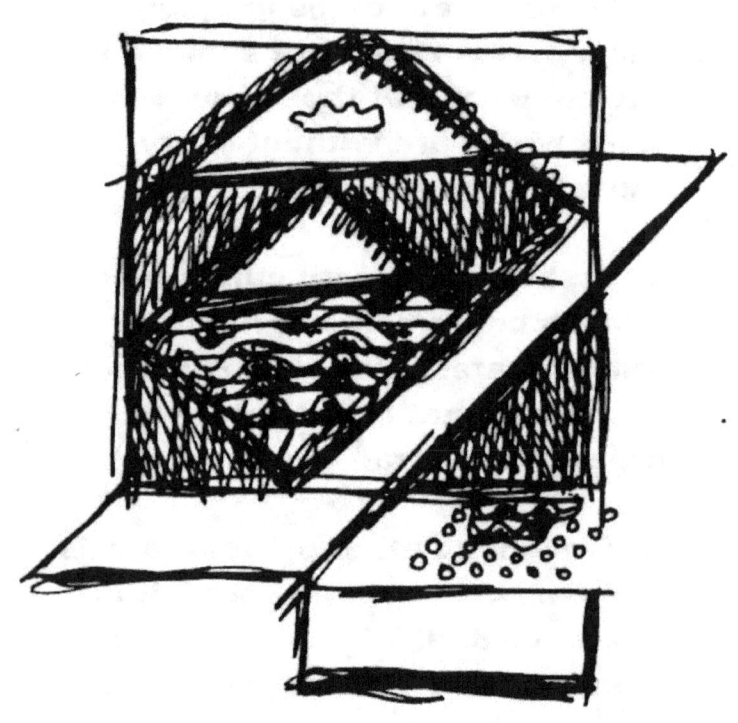

SUBLIMISM

One way to consider sublime art is in terms of landscape, and using properties of abversion.

One might call this, "seeing through the sublime eyes of a child".

Indeed, this form creates certain paradigmatic and sublime relationships, such as those in the illustration at left:

*The sky can be captured.
*One can walk on the air.
*The sea drains away into the sky.
*Nature and culture are combined.

However, in some ways this is only a précis, the smallest beginning, to a study of the sublime in art.

Nathan Coppedge

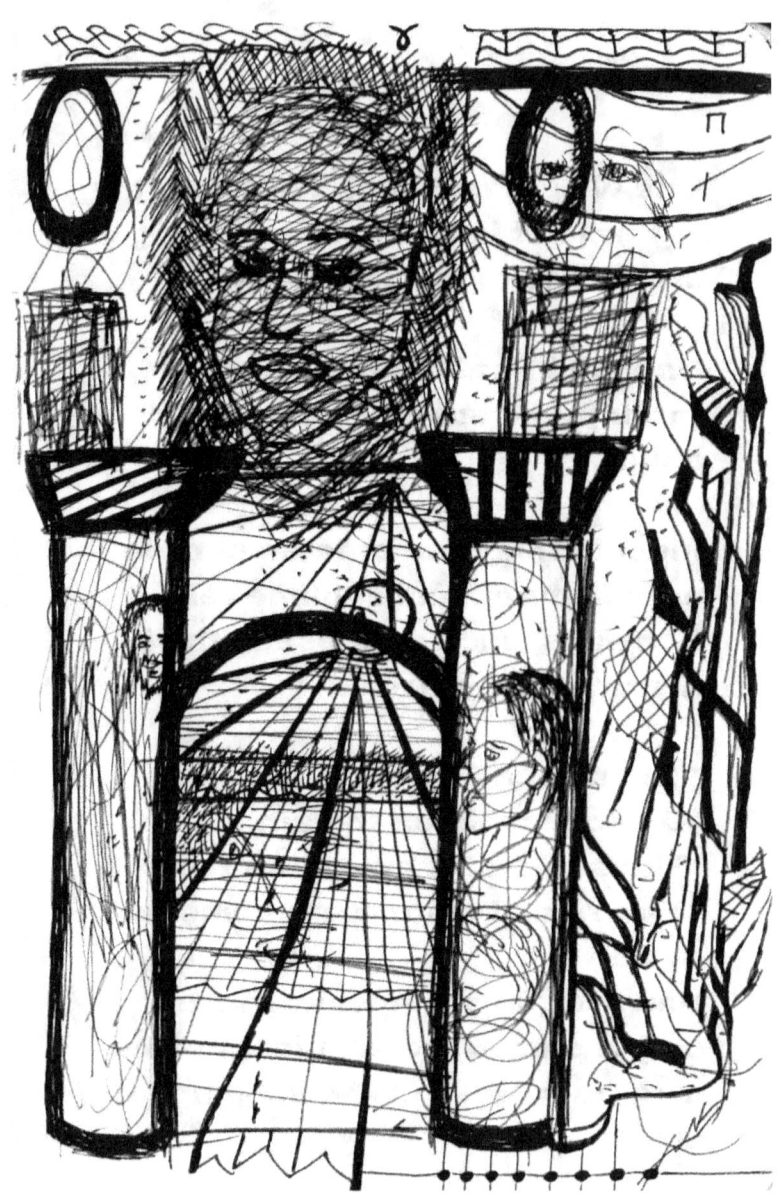

SUBLIMISM

Another approach, pictured here in a work by Nathan Coppedge from 2008, is to modify an adult landscape.

People, structures, patterns, and numbers come into play----

all to explain how life is an element of ART.

As perfect as this style seems, it is in fact difficult to maintain the energy necessary to convert the ordinary into the sublime.

Thus, most advanced sublimist techniques adopt a departure from the ordinary to explain how they are extraordinary.

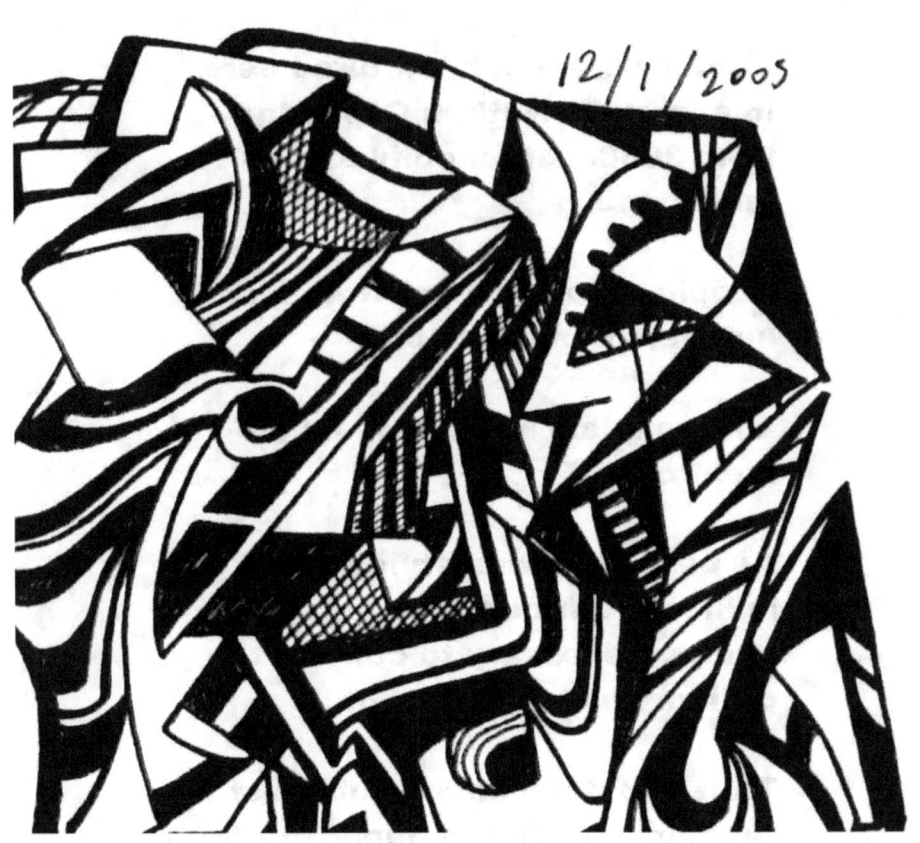

12/1/2005

SUBLIMISM

The genuine "sublime" in art may look something like this----psychic, unusual, with a sense of secret meaning.

One can easily see how an 'octopus woman', a syringe, a head serving as a house, an umbrella from a drink, and the texture of money might all get involved-----

Because each one connotes some sort of idea of the sublime.

To some extent, it is possible to just mishmash ideas, and get results. But it takes cleverness.

From another angle, all of those things add up to one thing (in this case): a kind of perfect composition.

Nathan Coppedge

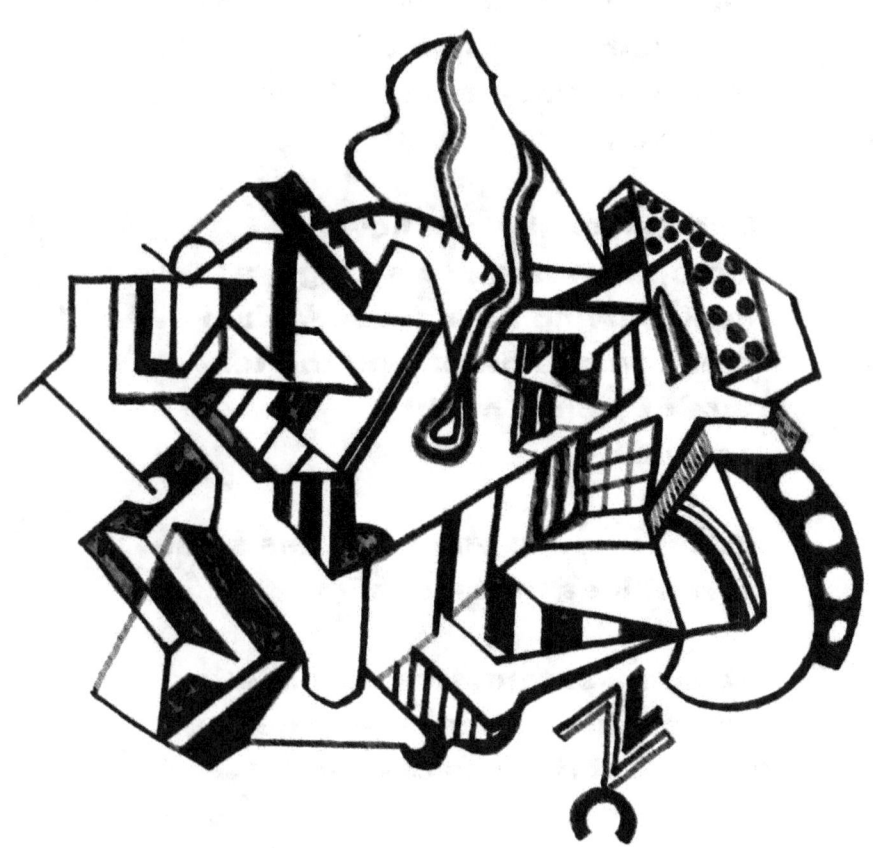

SUBLIMISM

A similar technique is effected here, without using an octopus woman.

Here we have simplified someone's hair to large, perspiration-like dots. We have adopted a motif similar to Dali's clocks, and introduced other stylized elements, like coins being inserted, a grid for a mouth, and an architectural bulkhead.

None of these elements detract from the work----

So it makes a good composition.

The stylized letters 'LRI' bring the composition together, but it is hard to tell what they stand for. They seem to follow some sort of aesthetic implication, rather than conscious sense.

Nathan Coppedge

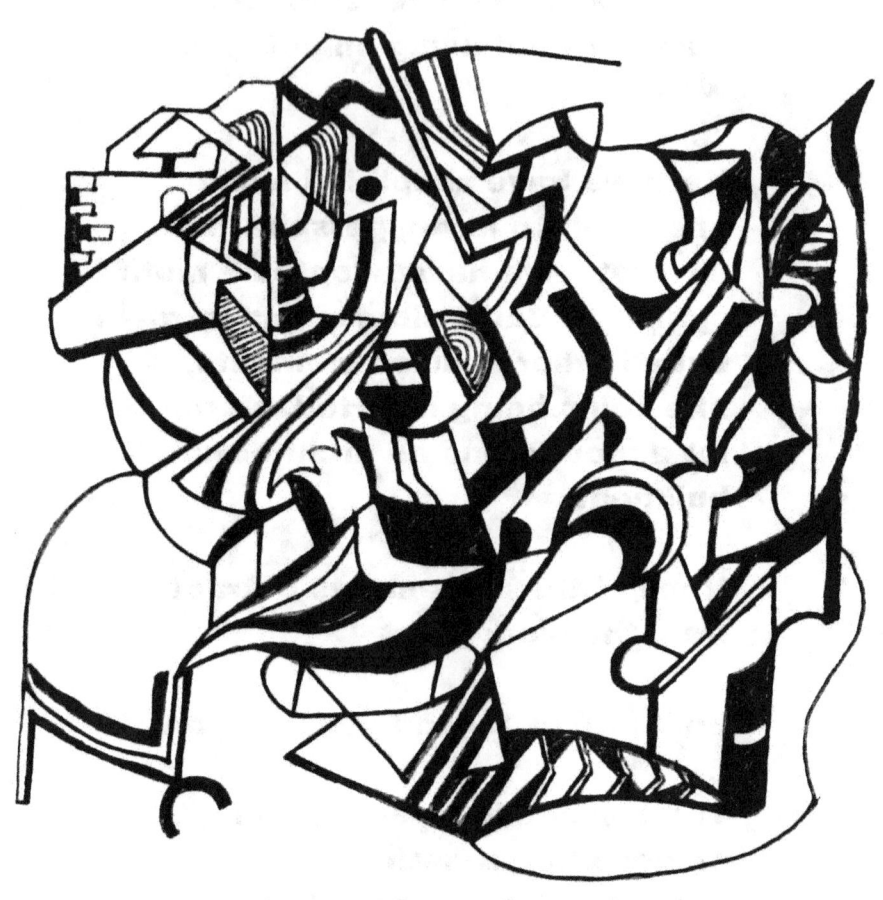

SUBLIMISM

In case you haven't noticed, the theme is learning from examples.

This piece is sort of like a mixture of the earlier two. It has elements that are architectural and abstract, as well as some technological or organic forms.

Notice how the architecture is being used to create a sense of depth and the beginning of textural variation.

However, in this case, the theme is so inspired and otherworldly that it is hard to draw a clear line as to where theory ends and sheer imagination begins.

As it turns out, that is an important distinction, as sublime artists may often be required to make epiphanical leaps.

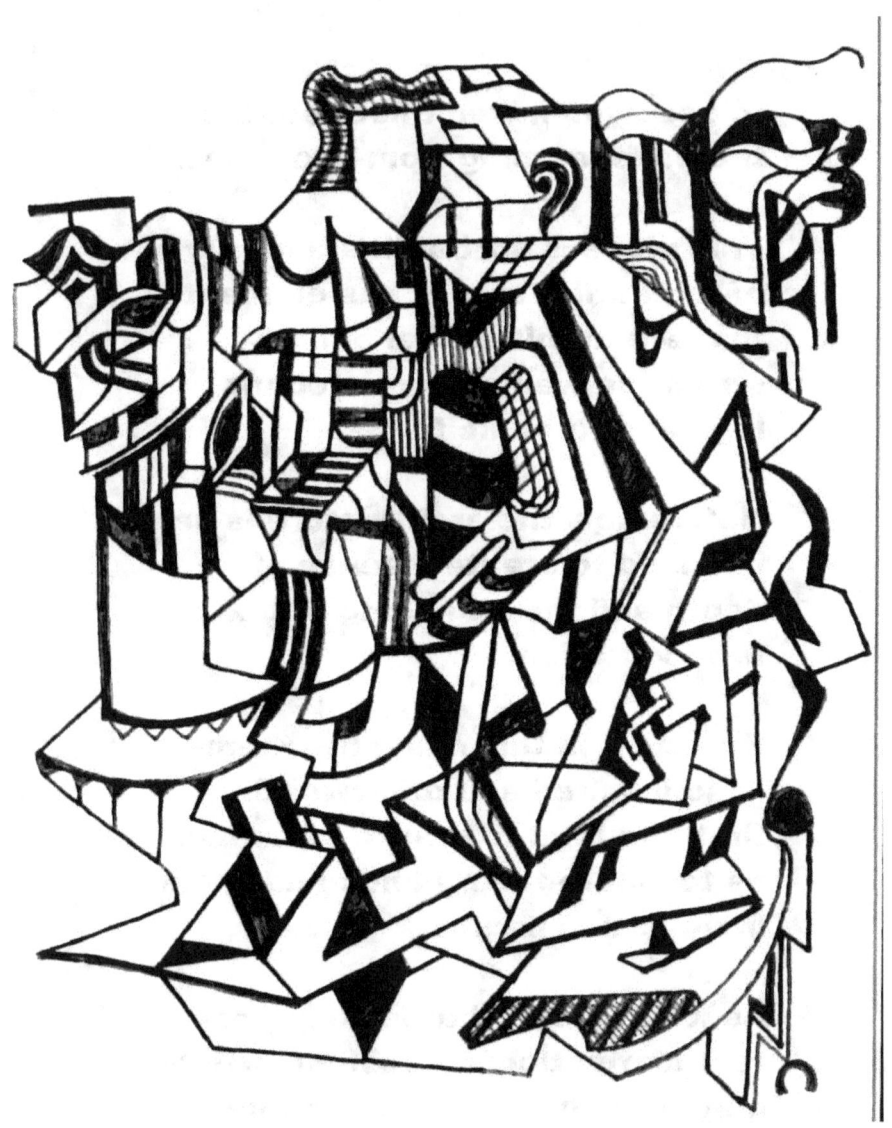

SUBLIMISM

Now that I have mentioned epiphanical leaps, it is worth mentioning one of the major avenues down which the sublimist might go:

He or she might technicalize until every single element follows its own rule!

To the left, we can see how breasts are becoming swiveling doors, hair has become a unique texture on top of the rest of it all, and various other elements are knotting and extruding.

This is not necessarily bad, but it is energy-intensive, as I mentioned for something else earlier, and also, it runs the risk of turning into an even more complex route, which grows ever more ersatz, as on the following page:

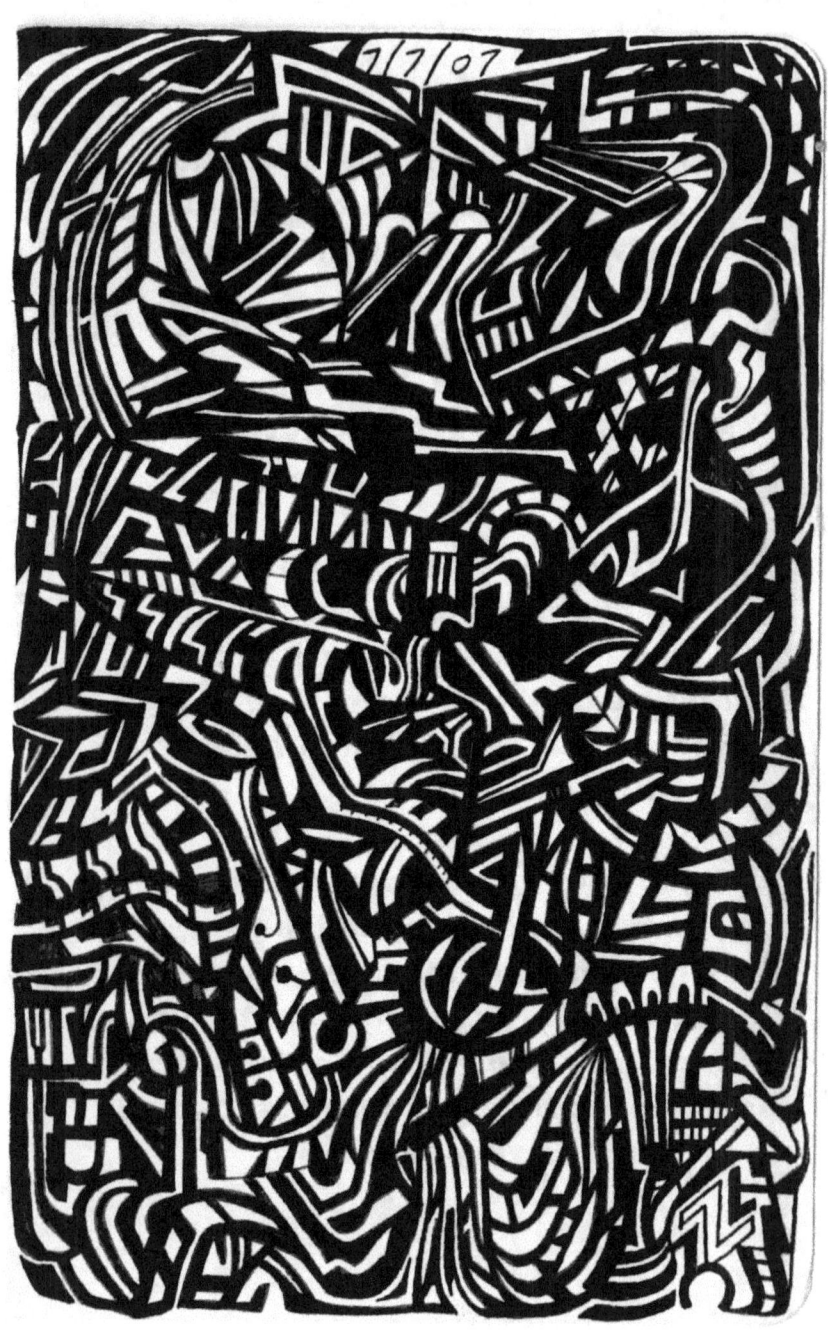

SUBLIMISM

HERE!

Sublime complexity reaches its zenith in works such as this...

But complexity is not necessarily the only property that should be improved.

Remember, more complexity requires more inspiration, and while that may not be a bad thing, it seems that working with smaller pieces may sometimes be more efficient...

Particularly if one is trying to learn something...

Nathan Coppedge

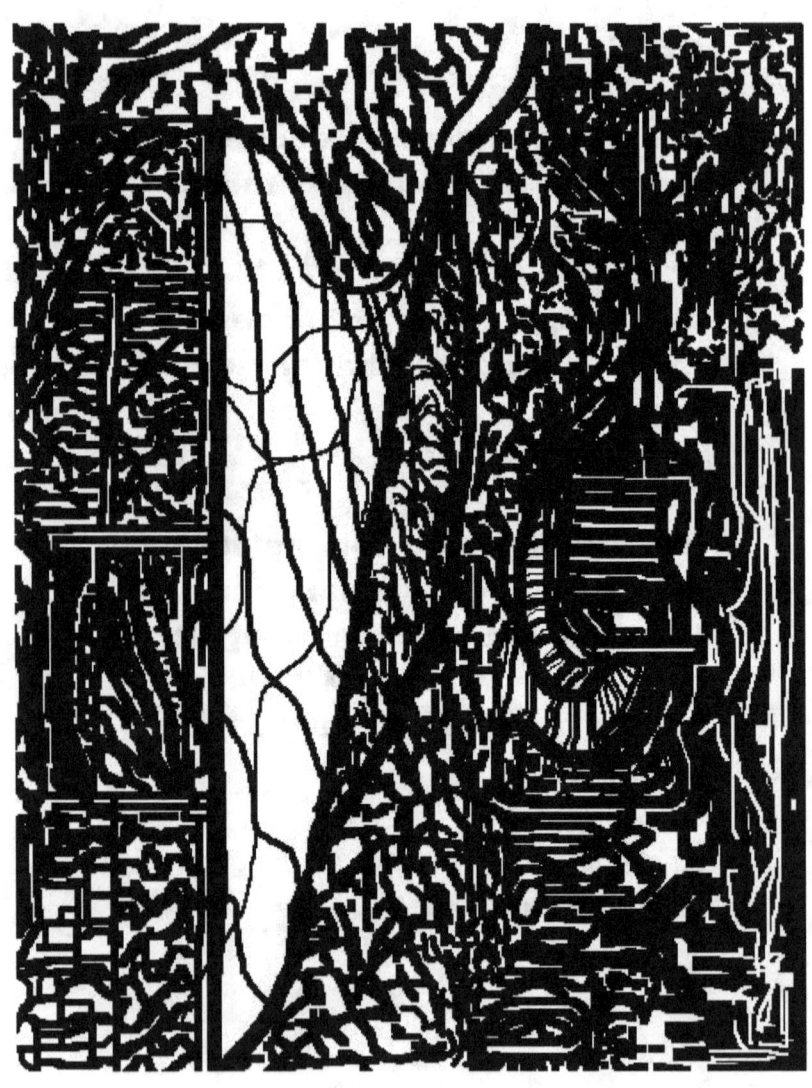

[above: A Sublimist Landscape]

SUBLIMISM

Another approach, I hinted to earlier, is to use landscape elements.

Thus, it is possible to define an entire aesthetic, through patterns and textures, ignoring the abstract option.

However, since getting a good result is still difficult, one might consider it more efficient to focus on abstractions, if the abstractions are original.

Generally, texture creates a lot of repetition which must be overcome by varying thematic elements.

Unless you want theme-oriented art, it is best to avoid texture theories as an exclusive option.

Nathan Coppedge

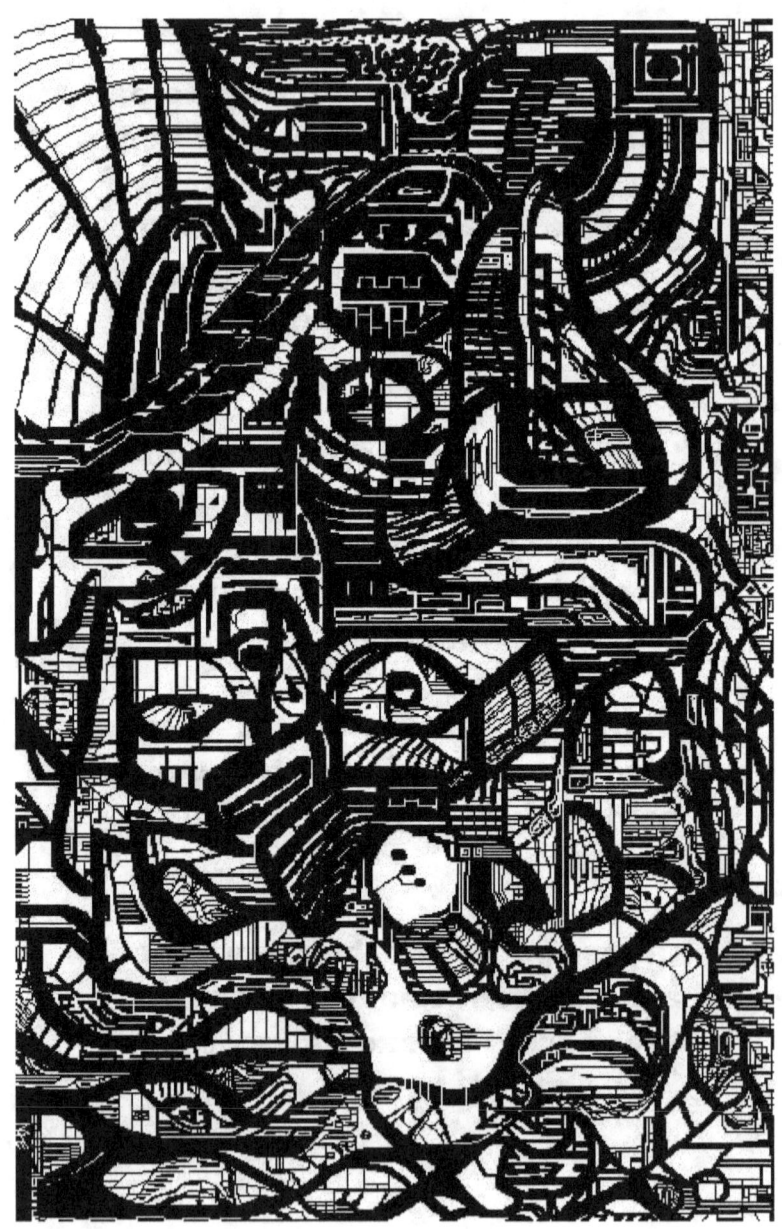

[side view]

30

SUBLIMISM

An exception to this is to use texture to define themes directly. In this way, themes can vary as much as the visual texture of the canvas.

However, this produces a kind of hodgepodge style which must be highly stylistic.

Depicted at left is Abstract 17, a digital work made painstakingly over the course of several weeks.

While the themes are sometimes grotesque, the sublime aspect allows an element of beauty.

Pouring water is a theme in several of my other works as well, creating a greater sense of unity.

Complexity and the black and white color scheme are also common in my other works.

Nathan Coppedge

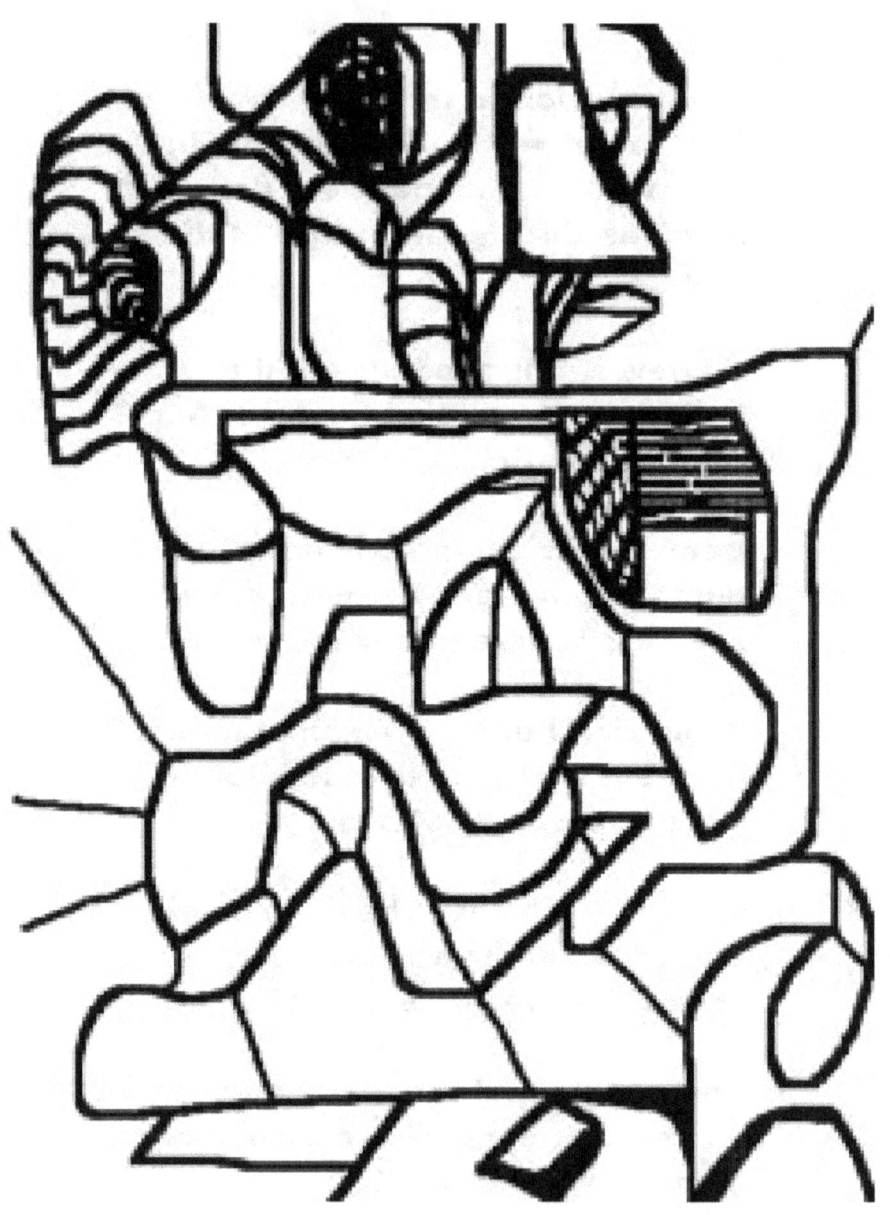

[side view]

SUBLIMISM

It is also possible to adopt a more outdoorsy approach, with less complexity.

I have found that this often involves toying with the use of lines and categories within the space.

For example, a river can be changed into a river of sand, thus permitting a use of parallel curving lines as a texture.

Rooms can be depicted as being outdoors.

Primary elements can be turned into abstract ones.

One part of the scene can mimic another part, with greater or lesser abstraction.

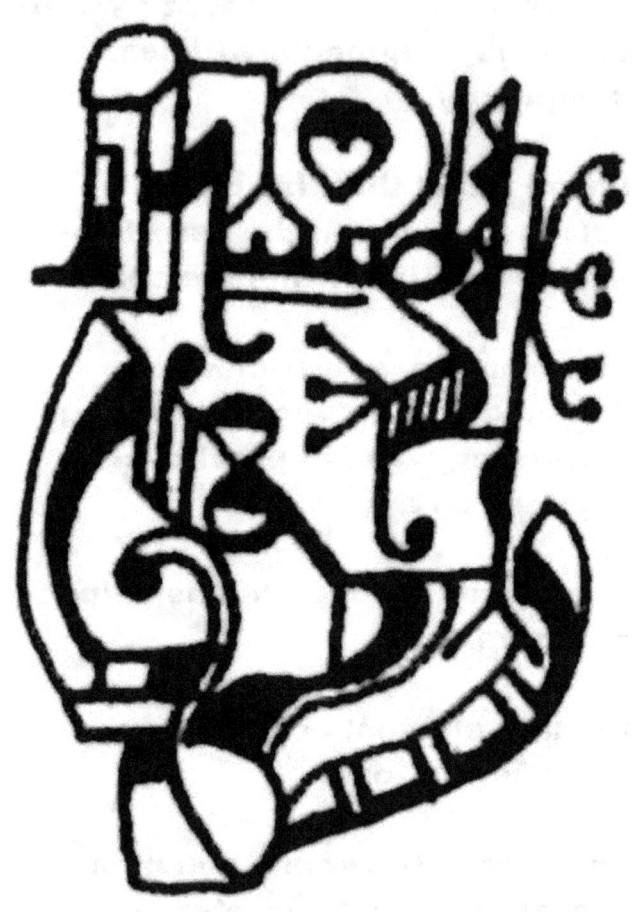

SUBLIMISM

Symbols can be introduced, either out of desperation, or as a way of organizing the structure of the piece.

Here, hearts have been played in normal and inversed positions, with forms variating the concept of a heart shape.

For example, the bird-foot symbol might be based on the phrase 'love birds'. And the hourglass might be about love 'standing the test of time'. The sideways candelabra seems to suggest a love that is optimistically more urgent than the need to hope.

Nathan Coppedge

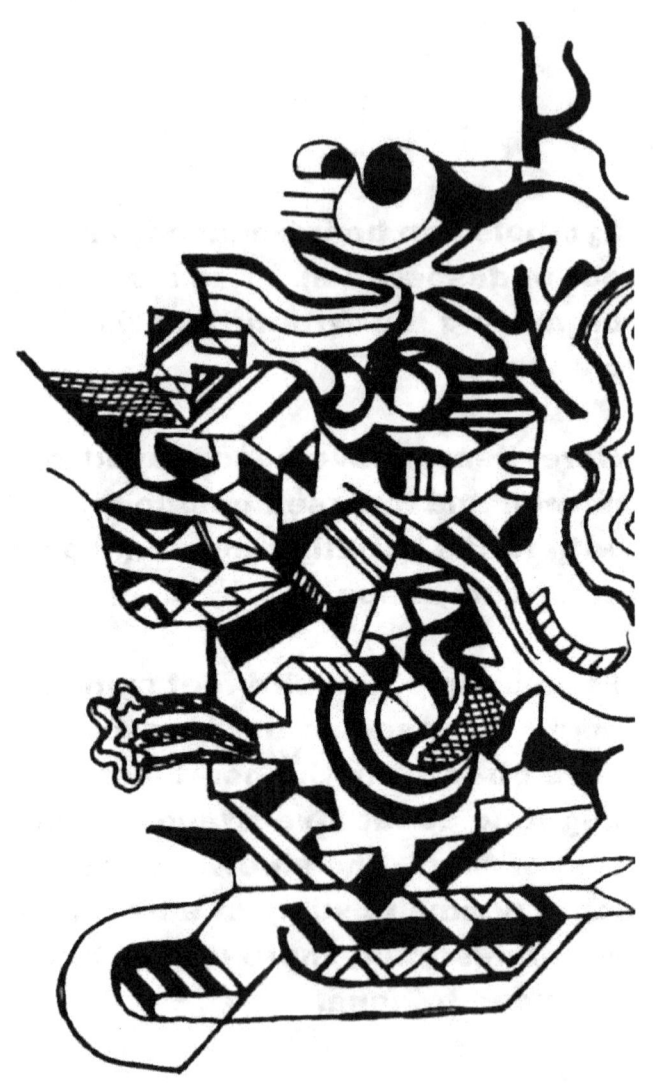

[side view]

SUBLIMISM

In some cases symbols and textures can be joined, creating unique compositions.

Special attention is paid to how formal properties, such as mathematical beauty or theories of aesthetic, determine the dimensionality of the elements.

Depicted here is a drawing called 'Verdun-NewVenice-Pandora' depicting Athena with the Baby Jesus, watching a waterfall pouring underwater.

Extreme, irrational thoughts can be used to create mental juxtapositions which are useful in deriving interesting or maddening mathematical properties.

The most beautiful formal elements in this piece are a pair of breasts, a dinosaur-like shape, and a withered fig tree.

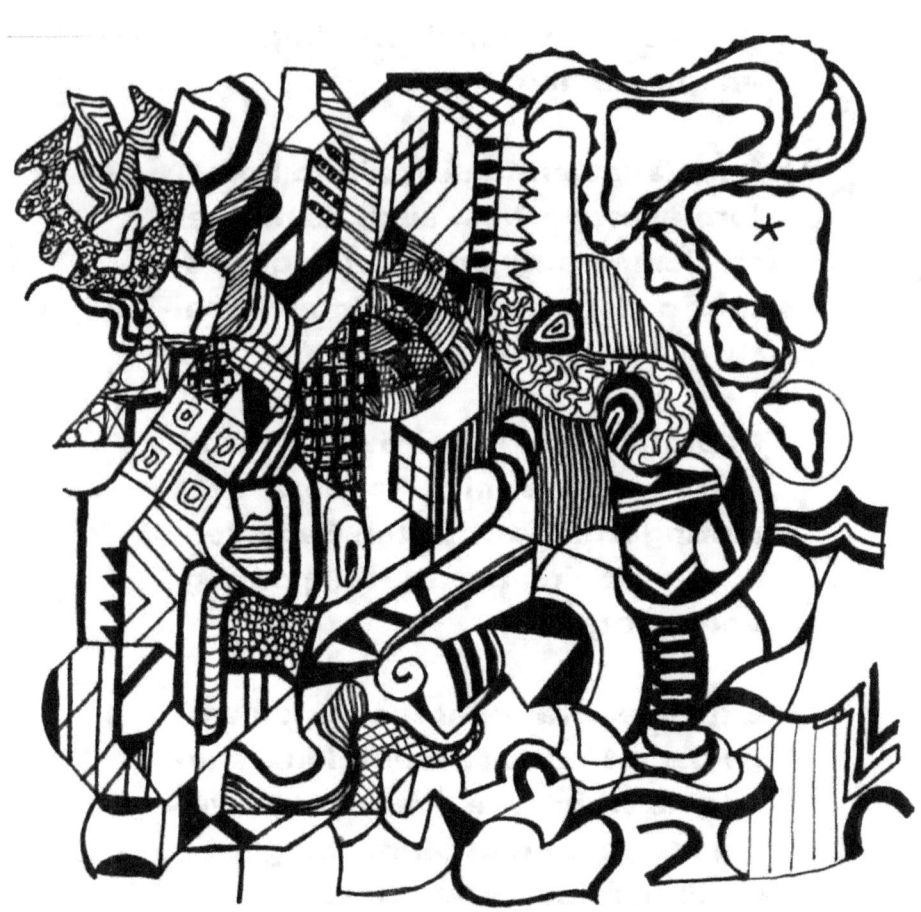

SUBLIMISM

In this piece, called simply 'Woodwork', I demonstrate the use of basic textural variation to perform a Sublimist aesthetic.

As usual in my work, the theme is less important than the direct effect on the brain.

The most beautiful aesthetic elements in this case are the triangles cut in the air by the saw, the alternating window shapes, and the portico exchanging a substance with the tree shapes.

Although highly grotesque, this piece has things to teach, not only in the use of many varied textures, but also in the overall aesthetic configuration. It is a study not only in abstraction, but in use of the imagination. It seems to ask the viewer to explore.

Nathan Coppedge

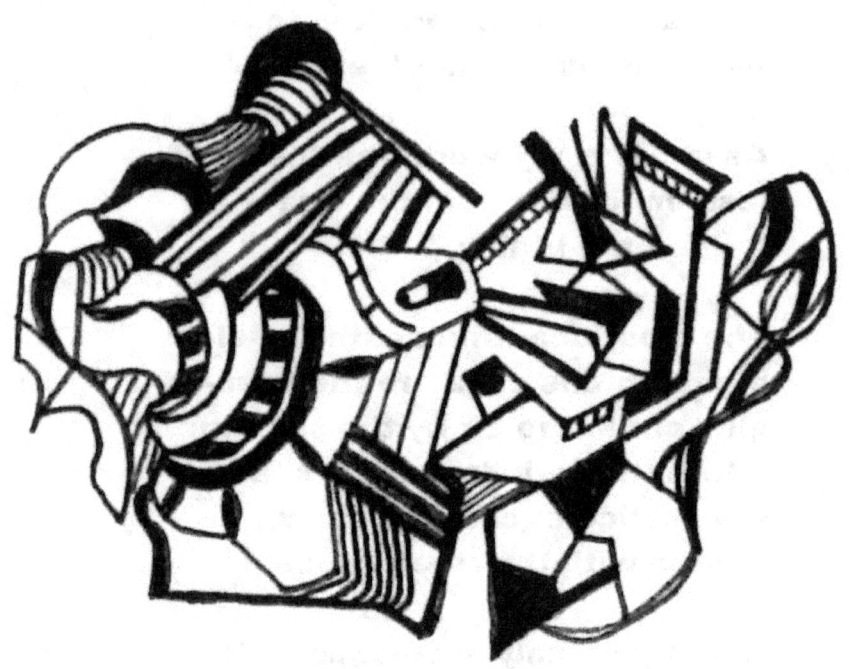

SUBLIMISM

Here a thematic element (someone laughing at someone) has been used to configure the entire canvas.

A critical attitude has been used, so that we see not only laughter literally destroying someone, but also a secondary level, specifically, a game, being played between the two corners of the paper.

Texture is used to show how one party is stronger, but the adventure is all the more interesting because half of the paper involves a disaster that can be explored by a little ladder.

The eyeballs ground the piece in an idea of suspension and disbelief, perhaps a way of mocking the one who laughed in the first place.

The effect is both dramatic and psychological.

Nathan Coppedge

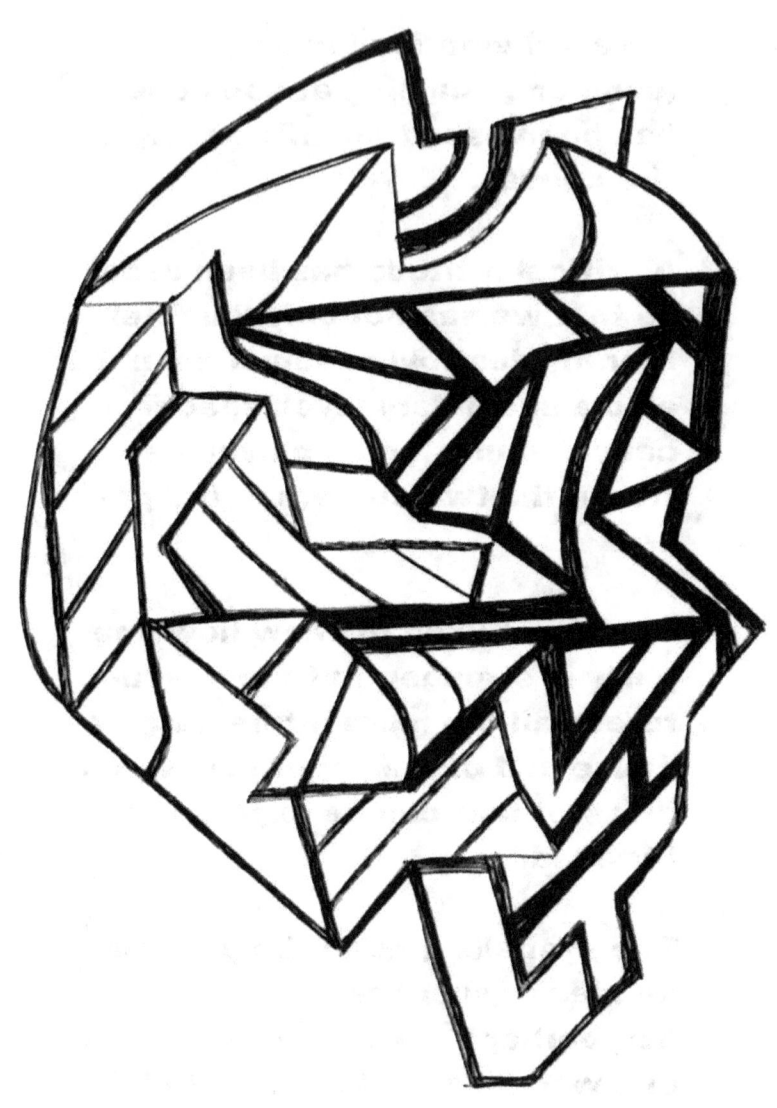

SIMPLE COMPOSITION SIX

SUBLIMISM

Overall, you may see how compositions reduce to formal thematic elements, which are not just themes in the sense applied to texture, but instead, themes of pure aesthetics.

Here, in Simple Composition 6, it can be seen that the conjoining of many different types of elements prefigures the concept of a sublime composition.

Later, as we look to other types of values, such as architecture and poetry, we would do well to notice how metaphorical the process of composition really can be.

Indeed, formal themes are the difficult virtue which prefigures any concept of a Sublimist composition.

Nathan Coppedge

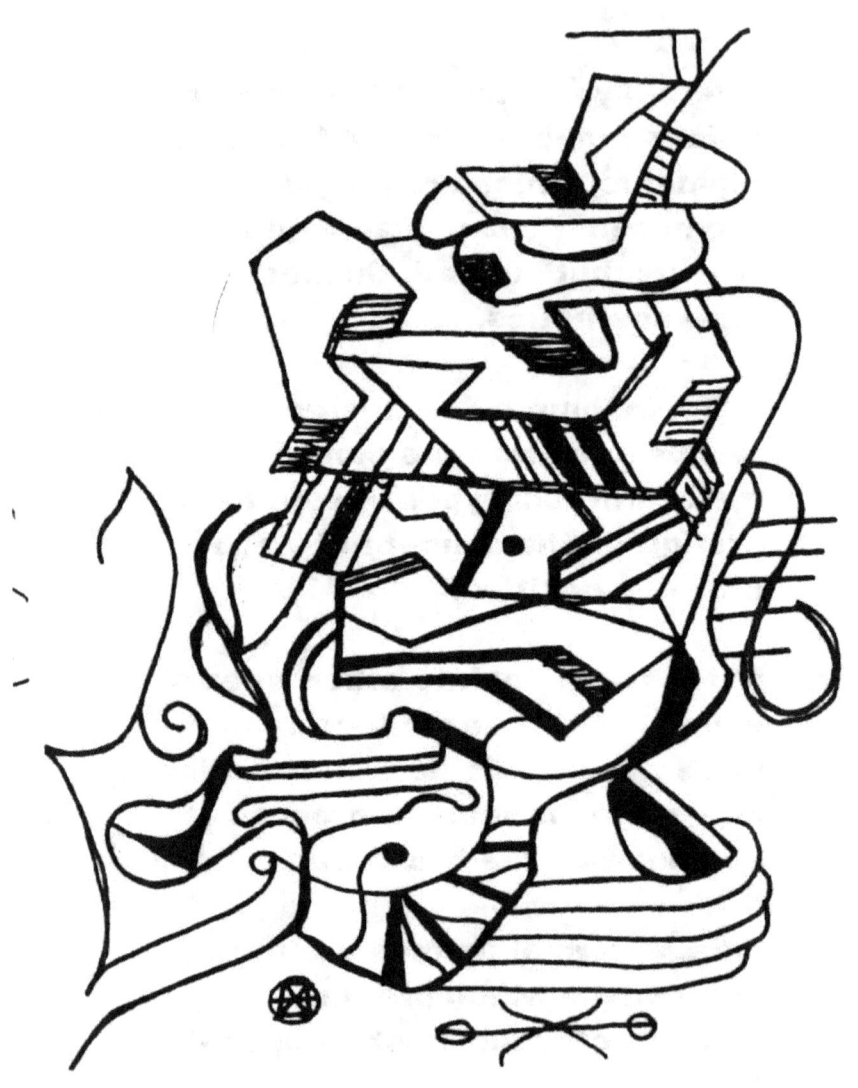

[SIDE VIEW]

44

SUBLIMISM

Of course, it is possible that specific elements are just as important as formal themes.

The creation of an archetypal objects plays the role of bridging the gap between formal themes and textural themes.

Specific elements may determine the exact impact of the work in the 'reader's' mind.

For example, a dimensional doorway can lead to a profound sense of perspective.

A jar that glints, or a stylized eye, or an open window can have a similar effect.

Elements like these grant a special eloquence to the artistic experience, an eloquence more easily acquired in poetry, although with a different set of requirements.

Nathan Coppedge

SUBLIMISM

ARCHITECTURE

Nathan Coppedge

SUBLIMISM

SUBLIME ARCHITECTURE, as I said, must adopt some additional formalisms on top of the minimal creative requirement of the visual arts.

The essence of sublimist architecture is therefore to formalize the most essential and three-dimensionally meaningful elements of the sublime aesthetic process.

I take this to be elements that include organic composition, perspective (most simply, windows and doors), and textural considerations effecting the mood of the viewer.

Sublime architecture is not just entertainment, it is also psychologically-grounded, and intense. Through this kind of purpose, it becomes intellectual, and coherent with other works of art.

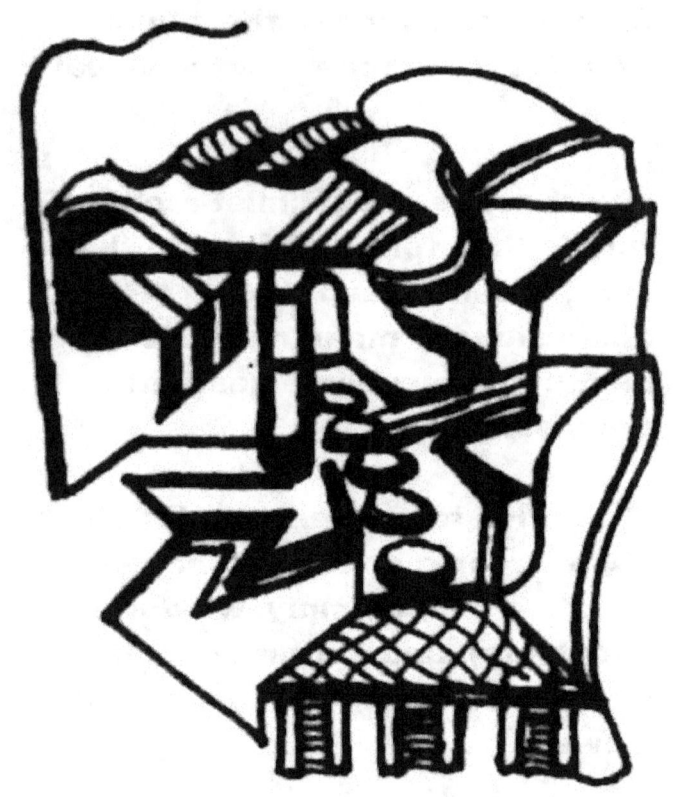

SUBLIMISM

A simple type of sublime architecture has learned to take advantage of the dimensions found in its context (usually three dimensions for architecture), and make purposeful use of those dimensions to achieve aesthetical aims, not only for the viewer, but for the occupant, the photographer, the artist, and other functional roles within the building.

Here we can see how dimensional elements prefigure a series of stepping stones.

The stepping stones create the sublime image of a typewriter, serving as a meta-function for the entire building.

E.g. : 'this building is writing' is more interesting than 'this is a house'.

This is just a basic thematic, and there are many others.

Nathan Coppedge

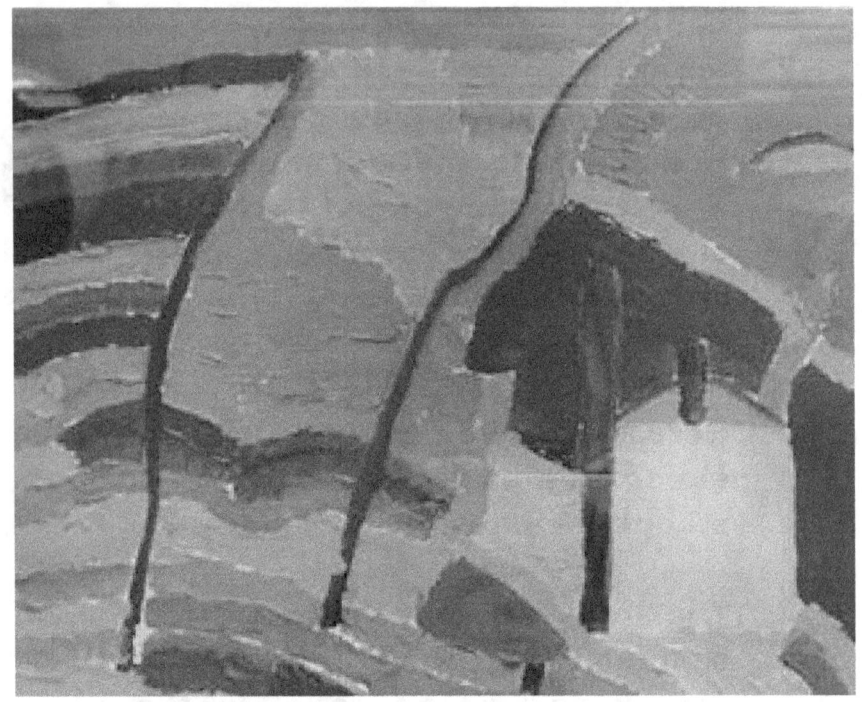

From 'Small House', by Nathan Coppedge.

SUBLIMISM

Another element to notice in the previous drawing are the stylized trees. Making use of stylized elements may mean manufacturing the background elements for a scene, in a manner not dissimilar to feng shui.

If trees cannot appear that way, it may be important to construct such things out of metal, or to build the house to suit the landscape.

However, when designing a sublime building, it is not just the landscape that counts. It is a hard lesson to learn, but there are organic versions of Georgianism and such which, through the use of organic elements, overcome some of the requirement for on-site planning.

Although inefficient through organics, they are actually efficient in terms of site.

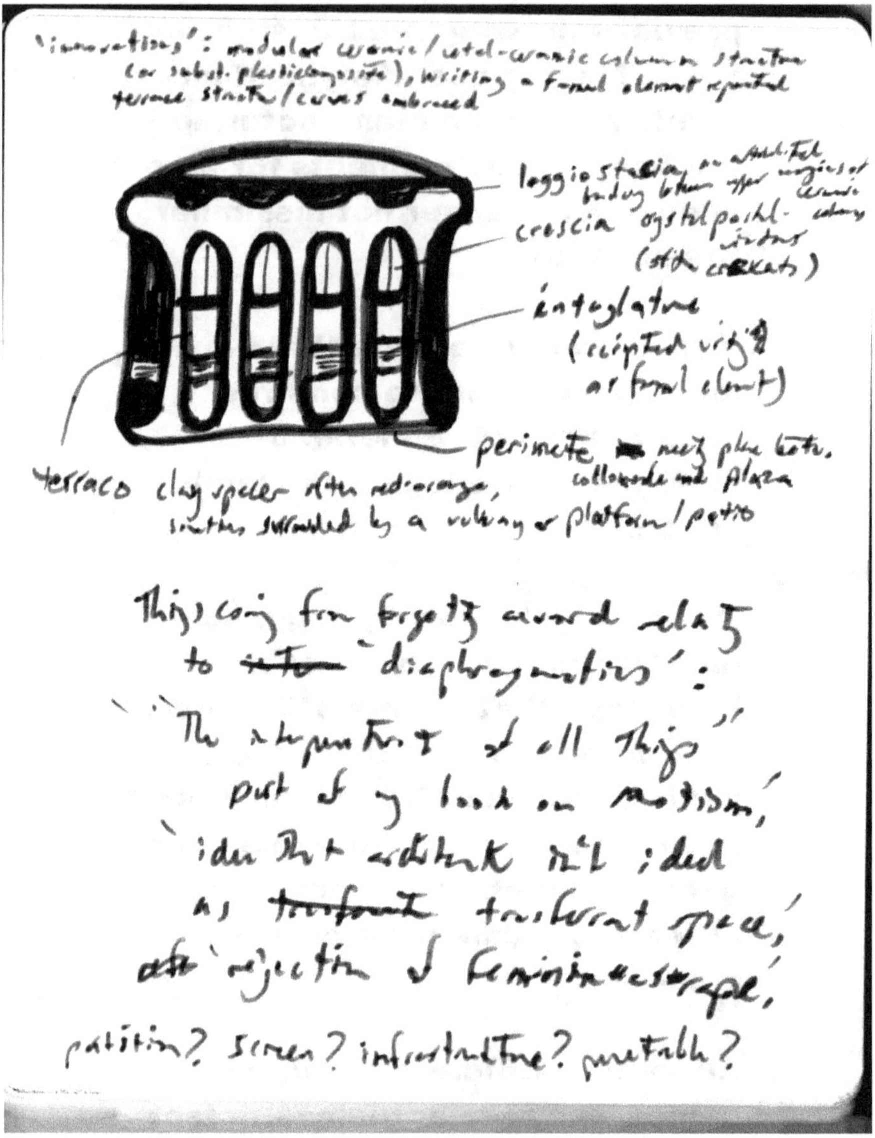
perimeter
terraco clay
diaphragmatics
"The ... of all things"
part of my book on ...
as ... space,
rejection
partition? screen?

SUBLIMISM

One of the primary forms of organic architecture is much like the page from one of my sketchbooks, dating from about 2005 - 2008.

The theme of vertical windows is extended into a similar cut-out shape for the corners, extending the modularization of design, and granting the proposed building a collegiate feel.

A rounded roof is used, not just to repel rain, but to unify the interior space and extend the ceramic or cement columns into an overall metallic carapace, of equal or better solidity.

The low point in the windows can be used to grant light to lower spaces, allow access through doorways, or to permit a view on the division between spaces.

Paradox - Key : Provision - Desire
Nature - Wall : Passage - Aspect

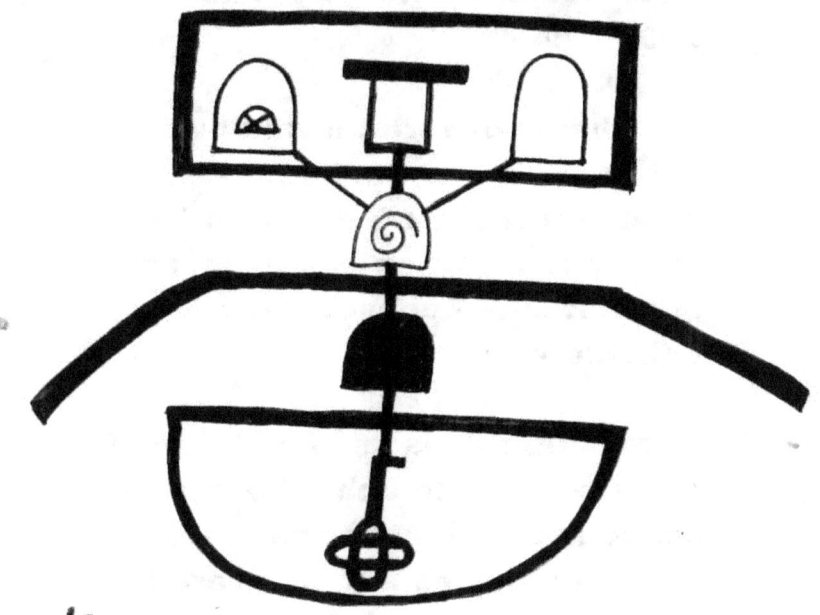

key,
Wall-if, Wall-of,
poisoned good
or
free passage,
disambiguated by falsehood

SUBLIMISM

In addition to the professional and sophisticated properties of architecture, there is also architecture in a more fun and philosophical sense.

Here depicted is a kind of maze, which is also a computation. The maze begins with a key or initiation, and ends with three options: (1) poison, (2) a blank wall, and (3) a corridor to the unknown.

This kind of diagram shows how if architecture is paradoxical, one might prefer the poison, which might mean anything. But if there is a theory involved, one might prefer a blank wall (metaphorical for structural principles, perhaps?), or freedom to explore many different design options.

The 'key', 'darkness' and 'confusion' are also relevant symbolism in the process, which can represent philosophy, working tools, etc.

Nathan Coppedge

SUBLIMISM

MORALITY

Nathan Coppedge

SUBLIMISM

Morality has been studied from many angles, but rarely do I hear it studied as something 'sublime'.

This observation offered a unique opportunity, to consider morality from a new vantage point, and thus, potentially, shed new light on ethical criticism.

The aesthetic ideal is not something by any means simple to apply to a moral quandary.

In fact, being honest, I was highly inspired to think of such a concept in any concrete terms. The inspiration was not only 'sublime' but 'morality' and 'sublime'.

So I am simply providing what I found as a notation, and forwarding it to any future thinkers who may happen to be interested in sublime morality.

Nathan Coppedge

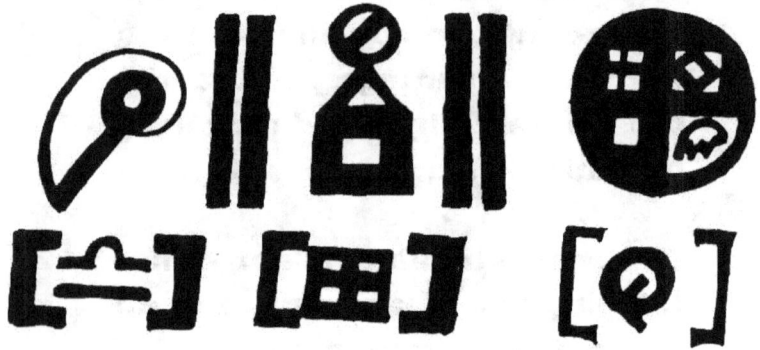

**[A diagram I drew around 2005.
I didn't initially know what it
meant, although I was sure it con-
cerned morality and categories].**

SUBLIMISM

VALUE SYSTEM - An attempt to summarize the objective value system, including some things that are Neo-Kantian or Utilitarian.

(1) One strives for the best thing, according to one's means: The Optimal.

(2) One judges according to one's authority over justice.

(3) It could be the wrong sock, then we put it on the wrong foot. Values are best equilibrated. The value of appropriateness.
One ought to apply a quality of justice, or some other principle, whenever one can: conditionals eke after justice or some higher principle. But the other rules come first.

---The above is taken from The Dimensional Justice Toolkit, an as-yet-unpublished work by Nathan Coppedge----

POETRY

Nathan Coppedge

SUBLIMISM

SUBLIMIST POETRY must evoke beauty while also containing an ideal which could be maintained by some mixture of genius and madness. It is not uneducated poetry, but if it cannot achieve pure and reasonable brilliance, then it must do this through devious means. One way that I have found is by relying on themes of madness.

Madness is a theme that has arisen numerous times in the Romantic tradition. Some even say that Blake's Tyger is an image of madness.

Whatever the case, poetry of this kind is an encounter with some sort of extreme, such as extreme beauty, or extreme thought. The extremity of the thing provides a motivator for the strength of the poem. Otherwise, education may be the strongest element of the sublimist tradition.

Nathan Coppedge

**These poems are supplemented
by a profound sense of process,
much like a visual artwork.**

SUBLIMISM

DO NOT FOLLOW IN THE FOOT-
STEPS, by Nathan Coppedge

Do not follow in the footsteps of
the master
master--
His garden is no humble pasture.

It is a place of wild magic, magic
or
it is laid barren.

Do not venture into that garden,
garden
its river has a bitter flavor
and its doors are guarded.

Do not go over the garden hedge
to find a woman or a monster--

Heaven is everywhere under the
sun
and hell is a road unguarded.

Do not go into the rabbit-hole
beneath the drinking moon
the tunnels there are fabulous
but there's an end to every one.

Nathan Coppedge

Do not go lightly into the
neighbor's yard,
and if there's no light, its better to
withhold.

Do not follow the sheep that
stray from every fold:
They're looking for a better cliff
to plunge, and leave this world.

Do not take heart of words that
are held
in shame
When the day is done a name is no
foul thing.

Across the frozen pond you may
have found another house
Let's say you flew and didn't fall,
or found a clever way around.

Even if you found a spouse
even if you found a happier home
would they welcome a wanderer
from the dark?

--April 23, 2006

SUBLIMISM

SWING by Nathan Coppedge

Under the preponderant clouds
wishing mist on the outskirts of cities
The crowd roves and raves
Speaking with the hearts of dead men
Wheezy with their instruments, the black
satin
leaves them standing on their own
besmirched with a sticky forgetfulness
wondering how it turned.
And, in another room
The men awake, as though just remember-
ing
A long voyage to the center of a thin rope
Somewhere in the clouds

--3/18/06

Nathan Coppedge

SUBLIMISM

UPON RETURNING TO A GARDEN
By Nathan Coppedge

Let's say that light was bone
And the skylark called
And the silver shone
And the madrigal
Of spring
Displayed like flowers
Hours forgotten;
Dark thestral forms that hold
The breath on the brink
Of another world
The sort of place where gardens
grow
And dials sunglazed
Wink at passing dragonflies
Copper beeches exploding
With that forgotten air

Nathan Coppedge

SUBLIMISM

***ESCAPE* by Nathan Coppedge**

I stopped calling things eachother
long before I knew
I'd found a way between the walls
where I might always go—
where I might go to sing—
to the remnants and the blooms,
sing of where and how I'd been
and would a day return—
moments where shadows grow
along each lonely thing.

Nathan Coppedge

SUBLIMISM

THAT HOUSE by Nathan Coppedge

I grew beyond the reaches of the floors
Beyond the bounds themselves bound
by their binded doors

I knew beyond the reaches of this house
lay one painted with a mingling paint
fastened against this new-found bitter-
ness.

And I grew, I grew to know
how others ventured still
beneath the eaves with timorous ear
or under shadows at the attic stair.
surrounded by the glutton of the house
espoused from stars, dignified from glass
growing empty in this faint distress.

I quit the word when I lay dear,
I quieted the noisy pause
that quickened my puppet heart
in the absence of an hour removed
from that flashing death of changing light

The quiet song lingers on my tongue
as though to linger on its quiet song
as though to sing quietly my lingering
as though to linger on my quiet, singing
how silence falls, and everything springs
up

SUBLIMISM

POETS, by Nathan Coppedge

What do we speak for those poets
reclining on luxurious shadows
clutching at the body of Venus
as though she begun every book?

Their lips pull at the glass
filled to the brim,
and fountaining with nectar.

Their brain pans are flowing with ink,
which dribbles from their eyes
and onto the pages of those
who are thirsty.

What do we speak of those lovers of
poets
their tongues warm with walking
words
their eyes mazy with the labyrinth
of the poetic spell?

What do we speak for the words
themselves,
their inky paws and tails
making every cat look black?

--April 22, 2006

Nathan Coppedge

SUBLIMISM

ADDITIONAL
WRITINGS

SUBLIMISM

ANALYTIC POSSIBILISM

The View held roughly by Elias Canetti, Novalis, Lichtenberg, Alexius Meinong, Quentin Meillassoux, and Nathan Coppedge.

Thoughts can have the properties of nature as a way of tasting nature.

There is no need for objective properties of nature, since properties are the senses. Truth can exist independent of the senses, and be expressed objectively in language via synthesis. Epicureans have a kind of knowledge which is practical, and evaluative.

Values define the content of truth. Nature, however, is more than sensory knowledge. It is Truth in a high sense.

Absolute knowledge is a hard bargain, but perhaps possible. Even so, we might accept that it is not automatically understood even in its true form.

It is possible to be absolute with language even without comprehension, and the truth of language is generally less real than the truths of nature, but also more valid for thoughts. Nonetheless, the truths of comprehension are supervened upon by the capacity to synthesize.

The mind is not external, although the eyes are.

Language is an approximation composed of labels that can be empirically tested.

It is the empirical test that constitutes proof, although at the same time it may be allegorized in language.

Language does not express the limitation of thought.

Nathan Coppedge

WRITING ON THE SPIRITS

I. Realization

There are many types of spirits, all of which behave willingly in relation to the Self. It is the goal of the Self to realize the spirits. (Drugs bring on false spirits). The anima is the soul of reincarnation. Psychology is the spirit of emotion. Sometimes stimulus leads to a fossil self which eventually becomes authentically born, through a fossil reality. The fossil is false, and yet the resulting spirit is true. The freedom of the mind to choose elements of the intellect maintains the authenticity of the Anima in conscious re-existence within the Fossil World. True spirit is partly pure Psychology, but it is also moreover the realization of the Many Spirits. Mana is the communication of spirit, and can become exaggerated if one's significance is not yet great. Great spirits can tolerate mana, often using it whimsically. Magical enchantment is the essence of location, and by having location, has no location. Enchanters are selfish and greedy in this respect, but also some of the best people and have renounced the False World, and are rewarded for this. Sorcerers enjoy the generosity of God, and have often abandoned sensation in favor of Mythical Psychology: the objective perception of Archetypes in their own Inherent Emotion. Sorcerers know the language of mythology, and have often been enchanters before. These truths seem hollow to those who have not yet perceived the vital root of their veridity.

II. Doubt

Ostensibly God already answered the only question we wouldn't know the answer to when he created existence!
 God was asking: 'What is nothing?' 'How can it be nothing?' 'What is divine about nothing?' Etc.
 Asking questions about nothing with a lot of power

84

SUBLIMISM

is like creating reality.

Alternately, you might believe that reality is eternal and the nature of consciousness is the unsolved question.

However, it is possible to see that consciousness is a means to an end to some extent. Highly expensive, often slightly disappointing.

As soon as consciousness seems to become cheap, it bears fruit. At that point we can define consciousness as paradoxical.

To the primitive tool-building brain all that consciousness needs is a reason to live, and some form of technicalism to mull into thoughts, or some equivalent thing to turn into emotions, or both, etc.

At this point you may find it is easier to understand consciousness.

Consciousness is holy, so far as that is possible. It is also an attempt to process the worst problems, and to find the best solutions.

I think I have heard someone define it as 'a holy paradox'. Other definitions could be proposed, often relating to the soul, transformation, attributes, powers, and modes of existence.

Nathan Coppedge

SUBLIME DETAILS

1. At the end, you say: we've come to the end of the end. Get it?

2. Upper: lower; Lower: higher (architecture).

3. This time, all that goes to waste! (magic shops that appear and disappear: is it better to buy or not?)

SUBLIMISM

FINAL NOTE:

I hope you enjoyed this volume, full as it is with themes of the sublime art, poetry, morals, and architecture. Read other books by Nathan Coppedge listed on the following pages, or feel free to write a review of those books you have already read!

Vive l' sublime!

BOOKS BY NATHAN COPPEDGE

Similar Books:

    **High Art: A guide to artistic
        Perfection
    Nathan Coppedge's Hyper-
        Cubism: post-cubist
        drawings and
        paintings.
    Book of Uniques**

Series:

**The Dimensional Encyclopedia
Perpetual Motion Genius' Guides**

Also Recommended:

**Fiction titles on the following
page.**

SUBLIMISM

**FICTION BOOKS BY
NATHAN COPPEDGE**

**The Dramatis Personae
One-Page Classics
Banned Classics**

**PSEUDONYMOUSLY
(BY MASTER KUO)**

**The Lessons of the Master
The Story of Master Wu**

BIO

Nathan Coppedge is a philoso-
pher, artist, inventor, and poet in
some capacity. He is the author of
over forty books, and has contrib-
uted to the Hyper-Cubist art move-
ment, which he calls the "second
iteration of Cubism". He has been
quoted in Book Forum and the
Hartford Courant, and is a member
of the International Honor Society
for Philosophy. A comment at The
Economist cites his possible influ-
ence upon economic policy in In-
dia. He cites his greatest accom-
plishment as the evidence he has
provided for perpetual motion, but
he also has devised methods of
philosophy which he hopes will in-
fluence future thinkers. He lives
alone in New Haven, CT.